故園畫憶

庚寅中秋

韩启德题

故园画忆系列
Memory of the Old
Home in Sketches

陕西古塔
Ancient pagoda in Shaanxi

高海平　绘画 撰文
Sketches & Notes by Gao Haiping

學苑出版社
Academy Press

图书在版编目（CIP）数据

陕西古塔 / 高海平绘画撰文. — 北京：学苑出版社，2021.5
（故园画忆系列）
ISBN 978-7-5077-6167-2

Ⅰ. ①陕… Ⅱ. ①高… Ⅲ. ①古塔—介绍—陕西
Ⅳ. ①K928.75

中国版本图书馆CIP数据核字（2021）第074405号

出 版 人：孟　白
责任编辑：周　鼎　康　妮
出版发行：学苑出版社
社　　址：北京市丰台区南方庄2号院1号楼
邮政编码：100079
网　　址：www.book001.com
电子信箱：xueyuanpress@163.com
联系电话：010-67601101（营销部）、010-67603091（总编室）
印 刷 厂：河北赛文印刷有限公司
开本尺寸：889×1194　1/24
印　　张：7.5
字　　数：160千字
图　　幅：140幅
版　　次：2021年5月北京第1版
印　　次：2021年5月北京第1次印刷
定　　价：60.00元

目　录

汉中市

榆林市

安康市

商洛市

Contents

Baoji City

Xianyang City

Weinan City

Yan'an City

Hanzhong City

Yulin City

Ankang City

Shangluo City

自 序

陕西是一个文化大省，同时也是一个美术大省。

陕西，简称“陕”或“秦”，为中国省级行政单位之一。传统上陕西分为三个区域，即陕北地区、关中地区、陕南地区。陕西历史文化厚重，陕西古塔更是在三秦大地遍地开花，其原因在于佛教文化在中国大地上的庞大影响力，尤其在唐、宋时期达到了巅峰。在陕西的大慈恩寺、荐福寺、大兴善寺、香积寺、草堂寺、青龙寺、卧龙寺等著名寺院中，均有佛塔的建设，并都完整地保留至今。我从古塔的考察中发现，以长安为中心的佛教文化辐射到了周围的渭南、铜川、延安、榆林、宝鸡、汉中、安康、商洛、咸阳等地，形成了大长安佛教文化圈；尤其是今西安周边的周至、长安、韩城、合阳、旬邑、山阳、耀州、富县等地的寺院建设水平之高，是有目共睹的。我带着虔诚的心态来绘制和诉说佛塔文化的博大精深，用绘画的方式来呈现佛塔艺术之美，也希望有更多的人来了解陕西的佛塔和其中蕴含的文化。

陕西有很多古塔，并且每一座古塔的形制设计与建造都不相同。根据陕西师范大学历史文化学院赵克礼教授的研究与考察，陕西境内现存古塔共 287 座。其中，南北朝 3 座、唐代 14 座、唐-宋 5 座、宋代 25 座、金代 1 座、元代 1 座、明代 96 座、明-清 12 座、清代 125 座、民国 5 座，分布在陕西省 10 个地市辖区的 76 个县区。从建筑材料上看，有砖塔 164 座、石塔 102 座、砖石塔 4 座、铁塔 5 座、土塔 10 座、木塔 1 座、琉璃塔 1 座，种类齐全、造型多样。唐宋时期，古塔主要集中在关中和陕北南部；明代，大型砖塔仍集中于关中，而陕北以佛塔居多；清代，风水塔、文星塔发展迅速；受元藏传佛教的影响，喇嘛塔、金刚宝座塔在省内也有分布。

作为一名美术工作者，我用脚步来丈量人类的历史与文化。三秦大地上的先民为后代遗留下了丰富的文化遗产，古塔就是其中的重要组成部分。我认为我有责任将其整理、绘制成一套相对完整的手绘画集来介绍给人们。本书的古塔专题考察与绘制，源于我大学本科时期对陕北、关中、陕南地区的实地考察。二十年的时间里，我几乎走遍了三秦大地的每一个角落，寻找着属于自己的创作素材。当然，我做得还很不够，这需要循序渐进地坚持考察。我继承了先辈们的治学方法，踏着前贤的足迹继续前行，在田野一线寻找着属于自已的艺术成果。引用一句屈原的名句:“路漫漫其修远兮，吾将上下而求索。”

在本书绘制的过程中，我一共收集并绘制了180余座陕西古塔，由于中途搬家，部分画稿遗失，现将部分做了重新补充绘制，并精选出140幅呈现给大家。有先后去过多次进行的现场写生，也有采访附近居民、摄影爱好者、文博专家后的记录描画。有的古塔考察，我在本科和研究生阶段就已做过多次调查和走访，并形成学术研究成果，散见各家报纸杂志，并有拙作出版发行，如《延安印象》《榆林印迹》《陕北村落彩绘考察》等。这些都给本书的绘制与写作提供了重要的支撑。特别需要说明的是，陕西师范大学教授赵克礼先生的专著《陕西古塔研究》，对我有重要的指导意义。书中的古塔信息与数据，给我以很大帮助。其著作是我的研究与行动指南，使我能够站在巨人的肩膀上继续登高望远。在此表示诚挚的感谢!

在互联网空前发达的今天，不少古塔爱好者的徒步考察成果，给我在寻找古塔的信息上提供了帮助，如“求是”的博客、“江河湖海四方客”的博客、华商论坛的“无为无级”和“碧山云叟的博客”等。他们对古塔的痴迷，让我看到，我只是爱好者中的一员而已，还要持续补课学习。感谢他们给我在考察路上和艺术创作上提供的帮助，以及诸多在幕后支持和帮助我的朋友们，在此表示诚挚的感谢!

是为序。

高海平

2019年11月20日于西安丰园居陋室

Preface

Shaanxi, abbreviated as “Shan” or “Qin”, is one of China’s provincial administrative units. Traditionally, Shaanxi is divided into three regions, namely, the Northern Shaanxi, the Guanzhong Basin and the Southern Shaanxi. Shaanxi has rich history and culture. The ancient pagodas blossomed in Shaanxi because of the influential Buddist culture, especially in the Tang (618–907 A. D.) and Song (960–1279 A. D.) Dynasties. In the famous monasteries in Shaanxi, many stupas have been built and are still intact. From my investigation of the ancient pagoda, the Buddhist culture centered on Chang’an has influenced the surrounding areas, formed the Great Chang’an Buddhist Culture Circle. I drew and wrote down the extensive and profound Buddhism pagoda culture with a pious attitude. I present the beauty of the stupa art by painting and also hope that more people would like to know more about the stupa in Shaanxi and its culture.

According to the survey of Professor Zhao Keli from the School of History and Civilization of Shaanxi Normal University, there are 287 ancient pagodas in Shaanxi. Among them, there are 3 built in the Southern and Northern Dynasties (420–589 A. D.), 14 in the Tang Dynasty (618–907 A. D.), 25 in the Song Dynasty (960–1279 A. D.), 1 in the Jin Dynasty (1115–1234 A. D.), 1 in the Yuan Dynasty (1206–1368 A. D.), 96 in the Ming Dynasty(1368–1644 A. D.), 12 in the Ming-Qing Dynasty (1368–1911 A. D.), 125 in the Qing Dynasty (1644–1911 A. D.) and 5 in the Republic of China (1912–1949 A. D.). They are distributed in 76 counties of 10 municipal districts in Shaanxi Province. From the perspective of building materials, there are 164 brick pagodas, 102 stone pagodas, 4 masonry pagodas, 5 iron pagodas, 10 earthen pagodas, 1 wooden pagoda and 1 glazed pagoda, with rich types and shapes.

Ancient pagodas are an important part of the rich cultural heritage created by the ancestors of Shaanxi. I convinced that I have the responsibility to sort and draw a relatively complete set of hand-drawings to people. The investigation data and drawing of ancient pagodas come from my field visits to the Northern Shaanxi, the Guanzhong Basin and the Southern Shaanxi during my undergraduate time. In 20 years, I have visited almost every corner of Shaanxi. In the course of drawing this book, I totally collected and drew over 180 ancient pagodas in Shaanxi province. However, part of them were lost because I relocated once. Now, I have made some supplementary drawings and carefully selected 140 of them to you. Among them, we can find on-the-spot drawings that have been done many times in succession field visits, as well as paintings according to records from neighborhood, photography lovers and cultural experts.

Zhao Keli, professor with Shaanxi Normal University, has given me great guidance in his monograph of " Research on Ancient Pagodas in Shaanxi", especially the information and data of ancient pagodas in the book, which have helped me a lot. I would like to express my sincere gratitude here! Nowadays, with the unprecedented development of the Internet, the field research results from many ancient pagoda lovers have become a source of information to me. I would like to express my sincere gratitude to them for their help in my research and artistic creation, as well as all my friends who have supported and helped me behind the scene.

Gao Haiping

Written in Fengyuanju, Xi'an on November 20, 2019

西安市

Xi' an City

新城区万寿寺塔

位于西安市新城区韩森寨西光中学南校区的操场上。又名藏经塔，建于明万历年间（1573年～1620年）。塔为六边六层楼阁式空心砖塔，通高22.26米。一、二层檐下雕有莲花、花草、垂莲柱等图案，三层南面有券龛。

Pagoda in Temple of Longevity, Xincheng District

Built during Ming Emperor Wanli's reign (1573–1620 A. D.), it is on the playground of the campus of Xiguang Middle School, Hansen Village, Xincheng District, Xi'an city. The pagoda is a hollow brick one with six-sided and six-storey, which is 22.26 meters high.

碑林区宝庆寺塔

位于西安市碑林区南门内、书院门街口北侧。又名宝庆寺华塔，寺初建于隋仁寿年间（601年～604年），塔始建于唐文宗时期（827年～840年），明景泰年间（1450年～1457年）重建于今址。塔为六边七层楼阁式实心砖塔，通高23米，砖龛内嵌有北朝和隋唐造像。

Baoqing Temple Pagoda in Beilin District

It is in the inside of the south gate, north of the street corner of the bookstore gate, Beilin District, Xi'an city, and was first built during the Tang Emperor Wenzong's reign (827–840 A. D.) and rebuilt during Ming Emperor Jingtai's reign (1450–1457 A. D.). the pagoda is 23 meters high, and its brick niches are embedded with statues of the Northern Dynasties (386–581 A. D.) and Sui (581–618 A. D.) and Tang Dynasties (581–907 A. D.).

碑林区荐福寺小雁塔

位于西安市碑林区友谊路西荐福寺内。又名荐福寺塔，建于唐景龙年间（707 年 ~ 710 年），历代均有修葺。塔为方形十五层密檐式空心砖塔，现残存十三层，塔刹已失，残塔通高 43.395 米。该塔是我国古塔建筑中早期密檐式塔的代表，与大雁塔齐名。

Xiaoyan Pagoda in Jianfu Temple, Beilin District

Built during the Tang Emperor Jinglong's reign (707–710 A. D.), it, which also called Pagoda in Jianfu Temple, is in Jianfu Temple, the west of Youyi Road, Beilin District, Xi'an city. The pagoda is a square fifteen-storey hollow brick one, and now it has thirteen-storey left. It is the representative of the early dense-eaves pagoda in China, as famous as the Dayan Pagoda.

未央区敦煌寺塔

位于西安市未央区汉城乡青西村。始建于西晋，明、清多次重修。塔为六边七层楼阁式实心砖塔，通高 16.09 米，下有青石基座，风化严重，壁砖上印有“敦煌塔砖”字样。该塔塔身一、三、五层均在东面有券门，三层门额砖雕有“白豪藏”三字，一至四层檐下均有瑞兽、二龙戏珠、牡丹等祥瑞图案。

Pagoda in Dunhuang Temple, Weiyang District

It is in Qingxi Village, Hancheng Township, Weiyang District, Xi'an city. First built in the Western Jin Dynasty (265–317 A. D.), the pagoda was rebuilt many times in the Ming (1368–1644 A. D.) and Qing (1644–1911 A. D.) Dynasties. The Dunhuang Temple Pagoda is a six-sided and seven-storey solid brick one, with a height of 16.09 meters and a bluestone base under it. It is severely weathered and its brick is sealed with the words " Dun Huang Ta Zhuan".

雁塔区大兴善寺塔

位于西安市雁塔区大兴善寺内，因寺院建在隋都城的靖善坊而得名。始建于晋泰始二年（266年）。塔二层以上为六边五层楼阁式砖塔，通高18米；有券门，门额砖雕“舍利塔”三字，内置佛像，表面均有佛龛。

Dagoba in Da Xingshan Temple, Yanta District

Built in the 2rd year of Jin Emperor Taishi's reign (266 A. D.), it is in Da Xingshan Temple, Yanta District, Xi'an city. The pagoda is 18 meters high and above the second floor of it is a pavilion brick one with six-sided and five-storey.

雁塔区大慈恩寺大雁塔

位于西安市雁塔区大慈恩寺内。又名慈恩寺塔，始建于唐永徽年间（650 年 ~ 655 年），历代均有修葺，是目前在西安唐长安城地面上保存最为完整的唐代建筑。塔为方形七层楼阁式空心砖塔，通高 64.839 米。塔内置唐太宗撰写的《大唐三藏圣教序》和唐高宗为太子撰写的《大唐三藏圣教序记》，均为唐代书法家褚遂良书写。

Dayan Pagoda in Da Ci'en Temple, Yanta District

Built during the Tang Emperor Yonghui's reign (650–655 A. D.), it, which also called Pagoda in Da ci 'en Temple, is in Da Ci'en Temple, Yanta District, Xi'an city. The pagoda, which has been repaired through the dynasties, is the most complete Tang building preserved in Xi'an currently. It is a square seven-storey hollow brick pagoda with a height of 64.839 meters.

长安区圣寿寺塔

位于西安市长安区五台乡圣寿寺内。又名应身大士圆寂塔，建于隋仁寿年间（601 年～604 年）。方形楼阁式七层空心砖塔，通高 29.2 米。塔的一、三、五、七层的南北两面及二、四、六层的东西两面各开拱券形门洞，塔壁面有柱、枋、斗拱等仿木结构。

Shengshou Temple Pagoda in Chang'an District

Built during the Sui Emperor Renshou's reign (601–604 A. D.), it is in Shenshou Temple, Wutai Township, Chang'an District, Xi'an city. The pagoda is a seven-storey hollow brick one with square pavilion type, which is 29.2 meters high.

长安区二龙塔

位于西安市长安区王莽乡土门峪西南山顶上，建于唐贞观六年（632 年）。传说曾有二恶龙缠斗于土门峪，搅得周边鸡犬不宁，故造此塔以镇之。塔为方形密檐式空心砖塔，现存六层，残高 17.73 米。

Erlong pagoda in Chang'an District

Built in the 6th year of Tang Emperor Zhenguan's reign (632 A. D.), it is on the southwest of the top of the mountain in Tumenyu Village, Wangmang Township, Chang'an District, Xi'an city. The pagoda is a square seven-storey dense-eaves hollow brick one with a residual height of 17.73 meters.

长安区兴教寺塔

位于西安市长安区杜曲镇西韦村兴教寺内。兴教寺内有三座塔，是唐代高僧玄奘法师及其弟子窥基和新罗弟子圆测的舍利墓塔，为中国现存最古老的楼阁式塔。玄奘舍利塔为五层楼阁式塔，其左右为窥基灵塔和圆测灵塔，均为三层，形制与玄奘塔略同。

Xingjiao Temple Pagoda in Chang'an District

It is in Xingjiao Temple, Xiwei Village, Duqu Town, Chang'an District, Xi'an city. There are three pagodas in Xingjiao Temple, Sarira Tomb Pagodas of Xuanzang, a respected monk in the Tang Dynasty (618–907A.D.), and his disciple Kuiji and Silla disciple Yuance, which are the oldest extant pavilion-type pagodas in China.

长安区兴教寺玄奘塔

位于西安市长安区杜曲镇西韦村兴教寺西侧塔院。建于唐总章二年（669 年），重建于大和二年（828 年）。为方形五层楼阁式实心砖塔，高 21 米。第一层塔身南面辟砖砌拱门，内有方室，供奉玄奘。北门镶嵌有唐开成四年（839 年）篆刻“唐三藏大遍觉法师塔铭碑”一通，详细记述了玄奘的生平事迹。

Xuanzang Pagoda in Xingjiao Temple, Chang'an District

Built in the 2rd year of Tang Emperor Zongzhang's reign (669 A. D.), it is in the west courtyard, Xingjiao Temple, Xiwei Village, Duqu Town, Chang'an District, Xi'an city. The pagoda is a square five-storey solid brick one with a height of 21 meters. On the south side of the first floor of the pagoda has a brick arch with a square room dedicated to Xuanzang.

长安区净业寺道宣律师灵塔

位于西安市长安区终南山北麓凤凰山。净业寺是中国“佛教八宗”之一“律宗”祖庭，寺外峰顶上有道宣律师舍利塔。道宣（596 年 ~ 667 年），15 岁出家，曾助玄奘翻译佛经。塔为六边五层密檐式砖塔，通高 6 米。一层正面有券门，以上各层各面均有券门，六角攒尖顶。

Daoxuanlüshi Ling Pagoda in Jingye Temple, Chang'an District

It is in Fenghuang Mountain, northern foot of Zhongnan Mountain, Chang'an District, Xi'an city. The Daoxuanlüshi Ling Pagoda stands on the summit of the mountain, outside of the Jingye Temple. Dao Xuan (596–667 A. D.) became a monk at the age of 15 and ever helped Xuanzang translate Buddhist scripture. It is a six-sided and five-storey brick tower with a height of 6 meters.

长安区香积寺善导塔

位于西安市长安区香积寺村内。始建于唐神龙二年（706年），是佛教净土宗门徒为纪念祖师善导而修建的。原为十三层密檐式空心砖塔，今残存十一层，高33米。塔壁斗拱方木结构，有券门，底层有清乾隆年间（1736年～1796年）题刻的“涅槃盛事”四字。

Shandao Pagoda in Xiangji Temple, Chang'an District

Built in the 2rd year of Tang Emperor Shenlong's reign (706 A. D.), it is in Xiangji Temple, Chang'an District, Xi'an city. The pagoda was built by the disciples of Buddhism's Pure Land School to commemorate its founder Shandao. At the beginning, it is a hollow brick tower with thirteen-storey and dense-eaves, while now, it remains eleven-storey with a height of 33 meters.

长安区香积寺敬业灵塔

位于西安市长安区香积寺东侧，与善导塔相望。建于唐开元十二年（724 年）。塔为方形五层楼阁式空心砖塔，通高 15.12 米，塔顶有石制塔刹，南有券门。

Jing Ye Ling Pagoda in Xiangji Temple, Chang'an District

Built in the 12th year of Tang Emperor Kaiyuan's reign (724 A. D.), it is on the east side of Xiangji Temple, Chang'an District, Xi'an city and faces the Shandao Pagoda. The pagoda is a square five-storey hollow brick one with a height of 15.12 meters.

长安区华严寺双塔

位于西安市长安区华严寺。始建于唐贞元十九年（803 年）。华严寺现存有两座砖塔：东塔为杜顺禅师塔，四面七级，高 13 米，塔上刻“严主”和“无垢净光宝塔”。西塔为清国师塔，六面五级，高 7 米，上刻“大唐清凉国师妙觉之塔”。双塔为唐中期建筑风格的重要实物。

Twin Pagodas in Huayan Temple, Chang'an District

Built in the 19th year of Tang Emperor of Zhenyuan's reign (803 A. D.), it is in Huayan Temple, Chang'an District, Xi'an city. There are currently two brick towers in the Huayan Temple. The eastern one is Dushun Zen Master pagoda, with four-sided, seven-storey and a height of 13 meters. The western one is the Qingguoshi Pagoda, with six-sided, five-storey and a height of 7 meters. The Twin Pagodas are important building to show the architectural style in the middle Tang Dynasty (763–840A.D.) .

长安区太乙宫天池寺塔

位于西安市长安区太乙镇蛟龙峪村。建于明正德八年（1513年）。塔为六边七层楼阁式实心砖石塔，通高20.3米。塔身高大，一层较高，其余六层檐有斗拱、门格、椽头等均为仿木结构。

Pagoda in Tianchi Temple, Taiyi Palace, Chang'an District

Built in the 8th year of Ming Emperor of Zhengde's reign (1513 A. D.), it is in Jiaolongyu Village, Taiyi Town, Chang'an District, Xi'an city. The pagoda is a six-sided and seven-storey solid masonry one with a height of 20.3 meters.

高陵区三阳寺塔

位于西安市高陵区鹿苑镇高陵中学内。又名昭慧寺塔、高陵塔，建筑年代不详。八边十三层密檐楼阁式空心砖塔，通高 53 米。塔有南北两券门，二层设假门，三层以上东南西北面均为券窗。

Pagoda in Sanyang Temple, Gaoling District

The pagoda is in Gaoling Middle School, Luyuan Town, Gaoling District, Xi'an city. It is also called Gaoling Pagoda with unknown construction date. It is a hollow brick pagoda with eight-sided and thirteen-storey, which is 53 meters high.

鄠邑区宝林寺塔

位于西安市鄠邑区太平镇绕湾村南山中。又名敬德塔，始建于唐开元年间（713 年 ~ 741 年），宋代重修。塔为方形七层楼阁式实心砖塔，高 16.98 米，底层边长 2.8 米，仿木斗拱椽头瓦垄，宋代建筑风格。

Pagoda in Baolin Temple, Huyi District

Built during the Tang Emperor of Kaiyuan's Reign (713–741 A. D.), it, which also called Jingde Pagoda, is in Nan Mountain, Raowan Village, Taiping Town, Huyi District, Xi'an city. The pagoda is a seven-storey solid brick one with a height of 16.98 meters and is Song (960–1279 A. D.) architectural style.

鄠邑区草堂寺鸠摩罗什舍利塔

位于西安市鄠邑区草堂寺内。建于唐代。塔高2.44米，底座呈圆形。该塔用玉白、青砖、墨黑、乳黄、淡红、浅蓝、赭紫、深灰等颜色的玉石雕刻镶嵌而成，俗称“八宝玉石塔”。造型以鸠摩罗什出生地新疆克孜尔山脉为原型，又刻莲花祥云环绕，体型虽不大但十分精美。

Kumarajiva Dagoba in Caotang Temple, Huyi District

Built in the Tang Dynasty (618–907 A. D.), it is in Caotang Temple, Huyi District, Xi'an city. The pagoda is 2.44 meters and its base is round. It is inlaid with different colors of jade, such as white, green, black, yellow, red, blue, gray and so on, so it is commonly known as the " the Stone Pagoda Inlaid with Eight types of jades", which is quite exquisite.

周至县大秦寺塔

位于西安市周至县楼观镇塔峪村。大秦景教寺是基督教传入中国后最早建造的寺院之一。唐时称基督教为“景教”，称罗马为“大秦国”，故该寺被简称为“大秦寺”。据考证该塔为宋代建筑。塔为八边七层楼阁式空心砖塔，通高40.9米，内空可登顶。塔内遗存有景教泥塑和古代叙利亚外文刻字多处，是研究古代中西文化交流史的珍贵资料。

Pagoda in Daqin Temple, Zhouzhi County

It is in Tayu Village, Louguan Town, Zhouzhi County, Xi'an city. Daqinjingjiao Temple is one of the earliest temples built after Christianity introduced into China. In the Tang Dynasty (618–907 A. D.), people called Christianity as "Nestorianism" and Rome as "Daqin", so, the temple is called "Daqin Temple" for short. According to research, the tower, built in the Song Dynasty (960–1279A.D.), is 40.9 meters high and can be gone up to the top of the pagoda from the inside.

周至县八云塔

位于西安市周至县城云塔公园内。又名瑞光寺塔，建于唐景龙二年（708 年）。方形十一层密檐楼阁式砖塔，每层之间有砖砌出檐斗拱，高约 42 米。该塔底层每面各有两朵阴湿的痕迹，每朵约 1 米见方，虽大旱也不干，远近引为奇观，因而得名“八云塔”。

Eight Cloud Pagoda, Zhouzhi County

Built in the 2rd year of Tang Emperor Jinglong's reign (708 A. D.), it, also called the Pagoda in Ruiguang Temple, is in Yunta Park, Zhouzhi County, Xi'an city. The pagoda is an eleven-storey square brick one with pavilion style, which is about 42 meters high.

周至县清凉寺塔

位于西安市周至县城西南15千米处广济镇黑凤山曹家滩村。又名黑山寺塔，始建于初唐，于1958年被拆除。塔为仿木结构楼阁式空心砖塔。

Pagoda in Qingliang Temple, Zhouzhi County

It is in Caojiatan Village, Heifeng Mountain, Guangji Town, 15 kilometers southwest of Zhouzhi County, Xi'an city. The pagoda, also known as the Pagoda in Heishan Temple, was built in the early Tang Dynasty (618–712 A. D.) and was demolished in 1958. It is a pavilion-style hollow brick one which looks like that it is built of wood.

周至县仙游寺法王塔

位于西安市周至县马召镇黑水峪口。仙游寺原位于马召镇黑河口，因修水库，迁至今址。建于隋仁寿元年（601年），是中国现存唯一一座隋代砖塔。塔为方形七层楼阁式空心砖塔，高34.56米，东南方向有券门，塔身逐层减高，叠层出檐，形制为密檐式塔。

Fawang pagoda in Xianyou temple, Zhouzhi County

Built in the 1st year of Sui Emperor Shouyuan's reign (601 A. D.), it, the only brick pagoda built in the Sui Dynasty (581–618), is in Heishuiyukou, Mazhao Town, Zhouzhi County, Xi'an city. Xianyou temple was originally in Heishuiyukou, Mazhao Town and it was moved to today's address due to the construction of a reservoir. It is a square seven-storey hollow brick one with a height of 34.56 meters.

周至县仙游寺守贞和尚墓塔

原位于西安市周至县黑河口，建于清，今已无存。该塔为守贞和尚的墓塔，三层密檐式实心砖塔，有佛龛。该图依据仙游寺博物馆旧影描绘而成。

Shouzhen Monk Tomb Pagoda in Xianyou Temple, Zhouzhi County

Shouzhen Monk Tomb Pagoda, originally in Heihekou, Zhouzhi County, Xi'an city, was built in the Qing Dynasty (1644–1911 A. D.), but now it is gone. The painting is based on the old picture in the museum of Xianyou Temple.

周至县仙游寺普同塔

原位于西安市周至县黑河口，今已无存。该塔对研究陕西古代喇嘛塔有着重要的参考价值。该图依据仙游寺博物馆旧影描绘而成。

Putong Pagoda in Xianyou temple, Zhouzhi County

Originally located in Heihekou, Zhouzhi County, Xi'an city, the pagoda, which is gone now, has important value for studying Stupa in ancient Shaanxi Province. The painting is based on the old picture in the museum of Xianyou Temple.

周至县仙游寺见明和尚墓塔

原位于西安市周至县黑河口，今已无存。为见明和尚的墓塔。该图依据仙游寺博物馆旧影描绘而成。

Jianming Monk Tomb Pagoda in Xianyou temple, Zhouzhi County

Originally located in Heihekou, Zhouzhi County, Xi'an city, the pagoda, which is gone now, is Jianming Monk Tomb one. The painting is based on the old picture in the museum of Xianyou Temple.

周至县昆山律师衣钵塔

位于西安市周至县楼观台森林公园景区内。又名刘钵仓衣钵塔，始建于清道光四年（1824年）。塔为六边三层楼阁式实心砖塔，高10米。每层塔角有砖雕斗拱，檐下有砖雕花草图案，攒尖顶。塔身下嵌楷书石刻塔铭、塔记各一方。

Kunshanlüshi Yibo Pagoda in Zhouzhi County

Built in the 4th year of Qing Emperor's Daoguang's reign (1824 A. D.), it is in Forst Park, Louguantai, Zhouzhi County, Xi'an city. The pagoda is a solid brick one with six-sided and three-storey, which is 10 meters high.

铜川市
Tongchuan City

王益区兴元寺塔

位于铜川市王益区高坪村。原址上有兴元寺，建于隋开皇十三年（593 年），现仅存塔。塔为六边六层多宝塔式石塔，高 3.4 米。塔基为六边形须弥座，塔身各面线刻有花卉、瑞兽等图案，塔刹已毁。

Pagoda in Xingyuan Temple, Wangyi District

Built in the 13th year of Sui Emperor Kaihuang's reign (593 A. D.), it is in Gaoping Village, Wangyi District, Tongchuan City. There is Xingyuan Temple on the original site and only the pagoda remains now. The pagoda is a stone one with six-sided and six-storey with a height of 3.4 meters.

印台区铜川塔

位于铜川市印台区。又名重兴寺塔，建于北宋年间。该塔依山而建，高约 15 米，仿木结构密檐式。塔身雕刻富丽，塔顶有铁刹，由仰覆莲座、覆钵、相轮和宝珠组成。塔内有梯，可登顶。

Pagoda in Chongxing Temple, Yintai District

Built in the Northern Song Dynasty (960–1127 A. D.), it is in Yintai District, Tongchuan City. The pagoda, located on the foot of a mountain, is a dense-eaves one, which looks like that it is built of wood. The body is carved magnificently and it can be gone up to the top from the inside through stairs.

耀州区神德寺塔

位于铜川市耀州区城北步寿原下的半坡上，建于宋代。砖仿木楼阁式结构，通高35米，底围25.04米。该塔刻画精美，建筑风格雄浑庄严。

Pagoda in Shende Temple, Yaozhou District

Built in the Song Dynasty (960–1279 A. D.), it is on the half slope of the Bushouyuan, north of the Yaozhou District, Tongchuan City. The pagoda is a pavilion-style one, which looks like that it is built of wood, with a height of 35 meters. It has exquisite sculpture with majestic architecture style.

耀州区柏树塬塔

位于铜川市耀州区柳林镇柏树塬村。该塔所在地为白寺遗址，今遗址仅存砖塔一座。塔为六边七层密檐式空心砖塔，高约10米，底边长1.67米。塔上有券龛棂窗菱花图案、假门，从风格看为宋代建筑的特征。

Pagoda in Baishuyuan Village, Yaozhou District

It is in Baishuyuan Village, Liulin Town, Yaozhou District, Tongchuan City. The pagoda is in the site of the Bai Temple, where only one brick tower remains. It, with Song (960–1279 A. D.) architectural style, is a hollow brick pagoda with six-sided and seven-storey, which is about 10 meters.

耀州区药王山石塔

位于铜川市耀州区，又名法海造像塔。原塔在铜川延昌寺，1981年移入药王山。方形十层实心石塔，高2.62米，系整块青石雕成。塔有刻线浮雕佛龛，塔身层层出檐，仿木结构。从艺术风格看为南北朝建筑特征。

Stone Pagoda in Yaowang Mountain, Yaozhou District

It, also called Fahaizaoxiang Pagoda, is in Yaozhou District, Tongchuan City. The pagoda, at first, was located in Yanchang Temple in Tongchuan City and then moved to Yaowang Mountain in 1981. It is a square ten-storey solid stone one with 2.62 meters, which carved by a single block of bluestone. From the perspective of its style, it was built in the Northern and Southern Dynasties (420–589 A. D.).

耀州区香山寺舍利塔群·天一禅师舍利塔

位于铜川市耀州区庙湾镇香山寺村。建于清代。塔为六边三层实心砖塔，高 4.7 米，塔顶有残损。香山为清代佛教名山。

Dagobas in Xiangshan Temple, Yaozhou District·Zen Master Tianyi Dagoba

Built in the Qing Dynasty (1644–1911 A. D.), it is in Xiangshansi Village, Yaozhou District, Tongchuan City. The pagoda is a solid brick one with six-sided and three-storey, which is 4.7 meters high. Xiang Mountain is a famous Buddhist mountain in the Qing Dynasty (1644–1911 A. D.).

耀州区香山寺舍利塔群·心贞舍利塔

位于铜川市耀州区庙湾镇香山寺村。建于清光绪年间（1875年～1908年）。塔为六边三层实心砖塔，高5米。须弥座题有“监院心贞塔”。

Dagobas in Xiangshan Temple, Yaozhou District · Xinzhen Dagoba

Built during Qing Emperor Guangxu's reign (1875–1908 A. D.), it is in Xiangshansi Village, Miaowan Town, Yaozhou District, Tongchuan City. The pagoda is a solid brick one with six-sided and three-storey, which is 5 meters.

耀州区延昌寺塔

位于铜川市耀州区赵家坡村。塔为六边密檐式实心砖塔，残存八层，高 18.62 米，底边长 2.2 米。该塔塔身一层西辟有券门，二层以上实心，二层南北有券龛，每层出檐都有砖仿木双抄斗拱。从艺术风格看为宋代建筑特征。

Yanchang Temple Pagoda in Yaozhou District

Built in the Song Dynasty (960–1279 A. D.) in terms of its style, is in Zhaojiapo Village, Yaozhou District, Tongchuan City. The pagoda is a six-sided and dense-eaves solid brick one with a height of 18.62 meters, which has only eight-storey left.

宝鸡市

Baoji City

凤翔县天台寺舍利塔

位于宝鸡市凤翔县红花铺红花沟村。建于清道光年间（1821 年～1850 年）。塔为六边三层楼阁式实心舍利塔，通高 3.5 米。

Dagoba in Tiantai Temple, Fengxiang County

Built during Qing Emperor Daoguang's reign (1821–1850 A. D.), it is in Honghuagou Village, Honghuapu Town, Fengxiang County, Baoji City. The pagoda is a pavilion-style one with six-sided and three-storey, which is 3.5 meters.

凤翔县南宗禅师塔

位于宝鸡市凤翔县姚家沟镇寺庙沟村，据塔上所题铭文建于明代。塔为喇嘛式石塔，通高 3.6 米。

Zen Master Nanzong Pagoda in Fengxiang County

Located in Simiaogou Village, Yaojiagou Town, Fengxiang County, Baoji City, it was built in the Ming Dynasty (1368–1644 A. D.) according to the inscription on it. The pagoda is a lama-style stone one with a height of 3.6 meters.

岐山县太平寺塔

位于宝鸡市岐山县城太平路岐山县实验小学院内，建于宋元祐三年（1088 年）。八边九层仿木楼阁砖塔，通高 28.2 米，底层边长 2.6 米。从第二层起，每层都隐出假窗及栏杆。整个塔身斗拱繁密、秀丽端庄，是宋代古塔建筑艺术中的代表性建筑之一。

Pagoda in Taiping Temple, Qishan County

Built in the 3th year of Song Emperor Yuanyou's reign (1088 A. D.), it is in Qishan County Experimental Primary School, Taiping Street of Qishan County, Baoji City. The pagoda is a brick one with eight-eave and nine-storey, which is 28.2 meters. The whole body has great number of corbel brackets with dignified style, which is one of the representative buildings among ancient pagodas in the Song Dynasty (960–1279 A. D.).

扶风县法门寺塔

位于宝鸡市扶风县法门镇。法门寺原名阿育王寺，因舍利而置塔，因塔而建寺。塔原为木结构舍利塔，唐贞观五年（631 年）重修，后历代均有修葺。塔为八边五层楼阁式塔，通高 71.679 米。各层盖铜瓦，转角处设铜斗拱，飞檐翘角下挂铜风铃。

Pagoda in Famen Temple, Fufeng County

It is in Famen Town, Fufeng County, Baoji City. The pagoda was orginally a wooden one, which was rebuilt in the 5th year of Tang Emperor Zhenguan's reign (631 A. D.) and has been repaired in all previous dynasties. It is a pavilion-style one with eight-sided and five-storey, which is 71.679 meters.

扶风县湋峰塔

位于宝鸡市扶风县赵家沟村，始建于清乾隆二十三年（1758 年）。八边九层楼阁式空心砖塔，高 24.8 米，塔基边长 3.1 米。塔为砖木结构，外为砖砌，内有四根通天木柱，中间架有七层楼条上墁木楼板，每层楼留有出入口，可以登临。

Weifeng Pagoda in Fufeng County

Built in the 23th year of Qing Emperor Qianlong's reign (1758 A. D.), it is in Zhaojiagou Village, Fufeng County, Baoji City. The hollow brick tower, with eight-sided and nine-storey, is 24.8 meters high. The pagoda is post and panel structure with bricks outside and four tall wooden pillars inside.

眉县净光寺塔

位于宝鸡市眉县政府大院内。又名凌云塔，建于唐代晚期。楼阁式方形七层砖塔，高 22 米，塔每边长 4.46 米。由于年代久远与长期风雨侵蚀，该塔已向北倾斜；自塔倾斜后，又被称为斜塔。

Pagoda in Jingguang Temple, Mei County

Built in the Late Tang Dynasty (836–907 A. D.), it is situated in the government compound of, Mei County, Baoji City. The pagoda is a pavilion-style seven-storey square brick one with a height of 22 meters. It has tilted to the north because of its long history, long-term wind and rain erosion.

咸阳市
Xianyang City

渭城区千佛铁塔

位于咸阳市渭城区北社镇西村。又名福昌寺塔，建于明万历十八年（1590 年）。该塔由纯铁铸成，方形十层，高 33 米，边宽 3 米，层层有窗门，南向中空，有楼梯可攀登。千佛铁塔工艺超群，保存完好。

Thousand-buddha Iron Pagoda, Weicheng District

Built in the 18th year of Ming Emperor Wanli's reign (1590 A. D.), it, also called Pagoda in Fuchang Temple, is in Xi Village, Beishe Town, Weicheng District, Xianyang City. The Pagoda is cast from pure iron with a height of 33 meters, which is superb in workmanship and well preserved.

兴平市清梵寺塔

位于兴平市北寺巷。又名保宁寺塔、兴平北塔，建于唐贞观元年（627 年）。塔为八边七层楼阁式砖塔，残高 38.6 米。

Pagoda in Qingfan Temple, Xingping City

Built in the 1st year of Tang Emperor Zhenguan's reign (627 A. D.), it, also called Pagoda in Baoning Temple, is in Beisi Lane, Xingping City. The pagoda is a seven-storey and pavilion-style brick one with a residual height of 38.6 meters.

彬州市开元寺塔

位于彬州市城内。俗称雷峰塔，始建于北宋皇祐五年（1053年）。八边七层楼阁式砖塔，通高47.84米。塔身造型繁复，带乳钉真假券门相间相错，檐下砖雕、椽头、瓦垄、斗拱均为仿木结构，气势恢宏，繁而不乱。

Pagoda in Kaiyuan Temple, Binzhou City

Built in the 5th year of the Northern Song Emperor Huangyou's reign (1053 A. D.), it, also called Pagoda in Bin County and commonly known as Leifeng Pagoda, is in Binzhou City. The pagoda is a seven-storey and pavilion-style brick one with a height of 47.84 meters, which body is complex but not showy.

三原县文峰寺木塔

位于咸阳市三原县安乐乡中王堡村。又名中王堡木塔，建于元大德七年（1303 年），明清均有修葺。四柱八撑三楼式，通高 15 米，顶上覆盖琉璃瓦，檐下施如意斗拱。该塔结构严整、造型别致，是陕西省现存唯一的木塔。

Wooden Pagoda in Wenfeng Temple, Sanyuan County

Built in the 7th year of Yuan Emperor Dade's reign (1303 A. D.) and repaired in the Ming (1368–1644 A. D.) and Qing (1644–1911 A. D.) Dynasty, it is in Wangbao Village, Anle Township, Sanyuan County, Xianyang City. The pagoda is 15 meters high with neat structure and unique shape, which is the only wooden one in Shaanxi Province.

泾阳县振锡寺塔

位于咸阳市泾阳县蒋路乡嵯峨山上。又名悟空禅寺塔，建于唐大中年间（847年～859年），明嘉靖年间（1522年～1566年）重修。悟空禅师，唐著名高僧。塔为六边五层楼阁式实心砖塔，残高13.3米。塔基、塔身一二层为石砌筑，二层以上为青砖砌筑。

Zhenxi Temple Pagoda, Jingyang County

Built during Tang Emperor Dazhong's reign (847–859 A. D.) and rebuilt during Ming Emperor Jiajing's reign (1522–1566 A. D.), it, also called Pagoda in Wukong Temple, is in Cragginess mountain, Jianglu Town, Jingyang County, Xianyang City. Zen Master Wukong is a famous monk in the Tang Dynasty (618–907 A. D.). The pagoda is a five-storey solid brick one with a residual height of 13.3 meters.

泾阳县崇文塔

位于咸阳市泾阳县城内。又名铁佛寺塔、文塔寺，建于明万历十九年（1591 年）。由尚书李世达（泾阳人）倡导修建，是中国最高的砖塔。平面呈八角形，共十三层，总高度 87.218 米。塔基至塔顶全用青砖砌成，底层为重檐式，在南向塔门上刻有“崇文宝塔”四字。

Chongwen Pagoda in Jingyang County

Built in the 19th year of Ming Emperor Wanli's reign (1591 A. D.), it is in Jingyang County, Xianyang City. The pagoda is the tallest brick one in China, which construction has been advocated by Li Shida, minister from Jingyang County. The plane of the pagoda is octagonal. It has thirteen-storey with a height of 87.218 meters.

乾县香严寺普通宝塔

位于咸阳市乾县灵源乡孝义村。又名樊村塔，建于明弘治十年（1497年）。方形五层楼阁式实心砖塔，残高约7米。该塔塔身每一层都有一佛龛，塔檐四角和斗拱均为仿木结构，塔刹无存。

Basic tower in Xiangyan Temple, Qian County

Built in the 10th year of Ming Emperor Hongzhi's reign (1497 A. D.), it is in Xiaoyi Village, Lingyuan Township, Qian County, Xianyang City. The pagoda is a five-storey solid brick one with a residual height about 7 meters. There is a niche on each floor of the pagoda. The four corner of the pagoda and the corbel bracket look like that they are built of wood.

礼泉县香积寺塔

位于咸阳市礼泉县烽火镇刘家村内。俗称薄太后塔，建于唐末宋初。七层楼阁式砖塔，高44米，塔内空心有楼梯可直通塔顶，造型秀丽、典雅。

Pagoda in Xiangji Temple, Liquan County

Built in the late Tang Dynasty (618–907 A. D.) and early Song Dynasty (960–1279 A. D.), it is in Liujia Village, Fenghuo Town, Liquan County, Xianyang City. The pagoda, with beautiful and elegant shape, is a seven-storey and pavilion-style brick one with a height of 44 meters.

礼泉县金龟寺普通塔

位于咸阳市礼泉县阡东镇。建于清康熙初年。八边十层砖塔，高 45 米，每边镶嵌的方石上刻有浮雕。每层出檐，上覆琉璃瓦。底层南面有门可进入塔内，内有木梯可供攀登。塔身保存基本完好。

Basic tower in Jingui Temple, Liquan County

Built in the 1st years of Qing Emperor Kangxi's reign (1662 A. D.), it is in Qiandong Town, Liquan County, Xianyang City. The pagoda is a ten-storey brick one with a height of 45 meters, which body is basically intact. There is a door to the south of the ground floor to enter into the pagoda and a wooden ladder in it can be climbed.

永寿县武陵寺塔

位于咸阳市永寿县永平镇裕丰村。据资料载武陵寺建于北魏，如今寺已废弃，只保留有塔。塔具有明显的宋代建筑特征。塔为八边四层楼阁式空心砖塔，高 27.5 米。构造繁复多变，华丽美观，为宋代建筑中的精品。

Pagoda in Wuling Temple, Yongshou County

It is located in Yufeng Village, Yongping Town, Yongshou County, Xianyang City. According to the data, Wuling Temple was built in the Northern Wei Dynasty (368–534 A. D.) and has been abandoned now. The Pagoda remained, has clear architectural features of the Song Dynasty (960–1279 A. D.). The pagoda is a four-storey hollow brick one with a height of 27.5 meters, which is a masterpiece of the Song Dynasty (960–1279 A. D.).

旬邑县泰塔

位于咸阳市旬邑县城的中学内。建于北宋嘉祐四年（1059年）。八边七层楼阁式砖塔，高56米，塔身六层。塔内中空，有木梯盘旋至顶，每层有拱形门洞，与长方形的假门相间。该塔构思精良、做工精细，对研究宋代建筑有重要价值和学术意义。

Tai Pagoda in Xunyi County

Built in the 4th year of Song Emperor Jiayou's reign (1059 A. D.), it is in the Middle School, Xunyi County, Xianyang City. The pagoda is a six-storey and pavilion-style brick one with a height of 56 meters. It is well conceived and built with fine workmanship, which is of great value and academic significance of studying the architecture in the Song Dynasty (960–1279 A. D.).

武功县报本寺塔

位于咸阳市武功县武功镇。又名武功塔，建于北宋宝元二年（1039 年），后历代均有修葺。楼阁式砖塔，高 39.66 米，塔上各层东南西北均有券龛和券窗。

Pagoda in Baoben Temple, Wugong County

Located in Wugong Town, Wugong County, Xianyang City, it, also called Wugong Pagoda, was built in the 2rd year of Northern Song Emperor Baoyuan's reign (1039 A. D.) and has been repaired in successive dynasties. The pagoda is a pavilion-style brick one with a height of 39.66 meters.

渭南市
Weinan City

临渭区庆安寺风宝塔

位于渭南市临渭区交斜镇东堡村。修建年代不详，北宋重修，明嘉靖年间（1522年～1566年）因地震而重建。塔为方形九层楼阁式空心砖塔，高30米，各层有券门。

Fengbao Pagoda in Qingan Temple, Linwei District

Built in unknown date, it is in Dongbao Village, Jiaoxie Town, Linwei District, Weinan City. The pagoda is a square hollow brick one with nine-storey, which is 30 meters high.

临渭区慧照寺塔

位于渭南市临渭区下集镇慧照寺。塔建于唐，北宋、明有重修。塔高30余米，塔基四层有力士石雕，造型生动姿态各异。塔身中空，顶有铜刹。

Pagoda in Huizhao Temple, Linwei District

Built in the Tang Dynasty (618–907 A. D.) and rebuilt in the Northern Song (960–1127 A. D.) and Ming (1368–1644 A. D.) Dynasties, it is in Huizhao Temple, Xiaji Town, Linwei District, Weinan City. The pagoda is 30 meters high, with hollow body and copper brake on top.

华州区蕴空禅师墓塔

位于渭南市华州区大明乡郝窑村，建于宋代。塔为方形三层楼阁式实心砖塔，高 8 米，底边长 2.2 米。仿木斗拱檐头，塔刹无存，建筑风格古朴秀丽。

Zen Master Yunkong Tomb Pagoda in Huazhou District

Built in the Song Dynasty (960–1279 A. D.), it is in Haoyao Village, Daming Township, Huazhou District, Weinan City. The pagoda is a square solid brick one with three-storey, which is 8 meters high.

韩城市党家村文星塔

位于韩城市党家村小学内，建于清雍正三年（1725年）。初为木塔，光绪三十年（1904年）重建为砖塔。塔为六边六层楼阁式空心砖塔，基座方形，每层檐下施砖雕仿木斗拱、额枋等，顶部为砖雕莲座托宝珠式塔刹。塔内有木梯，可登顶。

Wenxing Pagoda in Dangjia Village, Hancheng City

Built in the 3th year of Qing Emperor Yongzheng's reign (1725 A. D.), it is in the primary school, Dangjia Village, Hancheng City. It, at first, was a wooden one and was rebuilt as a brick one in the 30th year of Qing Emperor Guangxu's reign (1904 A. D.). The pagoda can be gone up to the top from the inside wooden ladder.

韩城市昝村塔

位于韩城市西庄镇昝村。塔为六边五层楼阁式空心砖塔，通高 18 米，底边长 1.84 米，底径 3 米。顶层檐角出挑檐下施砖雕斗拱、垂莲柱，塔刹已残。

Pagoda in Zan Village, Hancheng City

It is in Zan Village, Xizhuang Town, Hancheng City. The pagoda is a hollow brick one with six-sided and five-storey, which is 18 meters high.

韩城市鸭儿坡塔

位于韩城市新城区苏东镇鸭儿坡村。建造年代不详，从风格看为晚清至民国时建建筑。塔为六边两层实心砖塔，高 3.5 米。

Pagoda in Yaer slope, Hancheng City

Built in unknown date, it is in Yaerpo Village, Sudong Town, Xincheng District, Hancheng City. The pagoda is a solid brick one with six-sided and two-storey, which is 3.5 meters high.

韩城市赳赳寨塔

位于韩城市金城烈士陵园北端。又名圆觉寺塔，建于金大定十三年（1173 年），清康熙四十一年（1702 年）重修。塔为八角形砖砌空心塔，高 23.36 米，底径 7.36 米，底部为正方形塔座。

Jiujiuzhai Pagoda in Han cheng City

Built in the 13th year of Jin Emperor Dading's reign (1173 A. D.), it is in the north of cemetery of revolutionary martyrs, Jincheng Town, Hancheng City. The pagoda is an octagonal hollow brick one with a height of 23.36 meters.

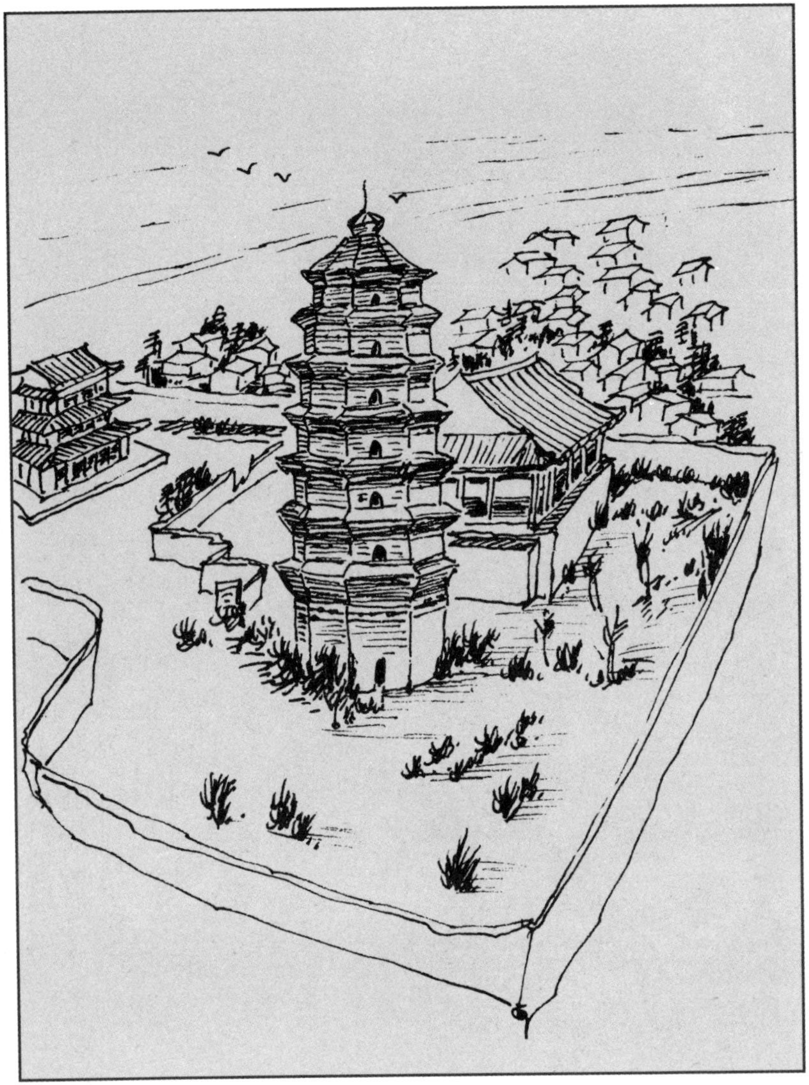

大荔县金龙寺塔

位于渭南市大荔县朝邑镇大寨子村东岱祠楼内。建于唐贞观元年（627 年），明弘治年间（1488 年～1505 年）重建。塔为八边七层楼阁式空心砖塔，通高 25 米。塔檐下有仿木砖雕斗拱，转角处饰斗拱垂莲柱，富有装饰感。

Pagoda in Jinlong Temple, Dali County

Built in the 1st year of Tang Emperor Zhenguan's reign (627 A. D.) and rebuilt during Ming Emperor Hongzhi's reign (1488–1505 A. D.), it is in the Baici Building, east of Dazhaizi Village, Chaoyi Town, Dali County, Weinan City. The pagoda is a hollow brick one with eight-sided and seven-storey, which is 25 meters high.

合阳县大象寺塔

位于渭南市合阳县东南杨家洼村，又名龙王庙塔、安阳塔，建于宋代。塔为方形十三层密檐式实心砖塔，高 28 米，底边长 4.6 米。塔身向东北方向倾斜已超过 5 度。

Pagoda in Daxiang Temple, Heyang County

Built in the Song Dynasty (960–1279 A. D.), it is in Yangjiawa Village, southeast of Heyang County, Weinan City. The pagoda, damaged now, is a solid brick one with thirteen-storey, which is 28 meters high.

合阳县百良寿圣寺塔

位于渭南市合阳县百良镇中学内。建于唐贞观年间（627年～649年），历代均有重修。塔为方形十三层密檐式实心砖塔，高31.73米。每层四边出檐，仿宫殿结构，四角均悬挂有风铃。塔顶方形，门额题“慈云洞天”四字。

Pagoda in Shousheng Temple, Bailiang Town, Heyang County

Built during Tang Emperor Zhenguan's reign (627–649 A.D.) and rebuilt in successive dynasties, it is in the middle school, Bailiang Town, Heyang County, Weinan City. The pagoda is a square solid brick one with thirteen-storey, which is 31.73 meters.

合阳县魁心塔

位于渭南市合阳县甘井乡北五中村内，建设年代不详。塔为六边七层实心砖塔，高 10 米，底边长 1.5 米。塔身无门，三层有一佛龛。

Kuixin Pagoda in Heyang County

Built in unknown date, it is in Beiwuzhong Village, Ganjing Township, Heyang County, Weinan City. The pagoda is a solid brick one with six-sided and seven-storey, which is 10 meters high.

合阳县千金塔

位于渭南市合阳县城关镇。又名白衣寺塔，系明万历三十七年（1609年）县城槐里人康守已为补合阳文脉捐银千两而建，故名千金塔。塔为八边十三层密檐楼阁式空心砖塔，高27米，底边长3.25米。

Qianjin Pagoda in Heyang County

Built in the 37th year of Ming Emperor Wanli's reign (1609 A. D.), it is in Chengguan Town, Heyang County, Weinan City. The pagoda is a hollow brick one with eight-sided and thirteen-storey, which is 27 meters high.

合阳县罗山寺塔

位于渭南市合阳县东马村。又名岱堡塔，建于唐。原塔为九层，现存残塔七层半，残高 30 米。该塔无底座，塔身直出地面，别具一格。

Pagoda in Luoshan Temple, Heyang County

Built in the Tang Dynasty (618–907 A. D.), it is in Dongma Village, Heyang County, Weinan City. The pagoda originally was nine-storey, and now it is only left with a residual height of 30 meters.

澄城县精进寺塔

位于渭南市澄城县东大街文化馆内。建于南唐时期，北宋庆历七年（1047 年）修复。塔为方形九层楼阁式砖塔，高 30.26 米，塔基周长 28 米。塔内中空，仿木结构，保存完好。

Pagoda in Jingjin Temple, Chengcheng County

Built in the Southern Tang Dynasty (937–975 A. D.) and repaired in the 7th year of Northern Song Emperor Qingli's reign (1047 A. D.), it is in the cultural center, Dongda Street of Chengcheng County, Weinan City The pagoda is a square nine-storey brick one with a height of 30.26 meters.

澄城县中社塔

位于渭南市澄城县交道镇中社村。又名卫塔，建于明成化年间（1465 年 ~ 1487 年）。楼阁式空心砖塔，高 22 米，底边长 5.3 米。内有壁画已残，有楼梯，造型简约大方。

Zhongshe Pagoda in Chengcheng County

Built during Ming Emperor Chenghua's reign (1465–1487 A. D.), it, also called Wei Pagoda, is in Zhongshe Village, Jiaodao Town, Chengcheng County, Weinan City. The pagoda is a pavilion-style hollow brick one with a height of 22 meters.

澄城县风水塔

位于渭南市澄城县安里乡三门村，建于清代。塔为六边六层楼阁式空心砖塔，通高27.5米，底径5.6米。底层南面有券门，二至五层有券窗、菱窗、梅花窗，六层无窗，攒顶置铁质宝珠式塔刹。

Fengshui Pagoda in Chengcheng County

Built in the Qing Dynasty (1644–1911 A. D.), it is in Sanmen Village, Anli Township, Chengcheng County, Weinan City. The pagoda is a hollow brick one with six-sided and six-storey, which is 27.5 meters high.

澄城县秀峰塔

位于渭南市澄城县安里镇张卓村。建设年代不详，清代重修。塔为六边五层楼阁式空心砖塔，塔高 23 米，底径 5.4 米。

Xiufeng Pagoda in Chengcheng County

Built in unknown date and rebuilt in the Qing Dynasty (1644–1911 A. D.), it is in Zhangzhuo Village, Anli Town, Chengcheng County, Weinan City. The pagoda is a hollow brick one with six-sided and five-storey, which is 23 meters.

蒲城县北寺宝塔

位于渭南市蒲城县，建于北宋绍圣三年（1096 年）。由当地人王信捐资修建，系原崇寿寺舍利宝塔，塔为方形十三级密檐式空心砖塔，高 47 米。

Beisi Pagoda in Pucheng County

Built in the 3th year of Song Emperor Shaosheng's reign (1096 A. D.), it is in Pucheng County, Weinan City. Funded by local people Wang Xin, the pagoda is the former sarira pagoda in Chongshou Temple, which is 47 meters high.

蒲城县慧彻寺舍利塔

位于渭南市蒲城县蒲城中学内。俗称南寺唐塔，建于唐贞观元年（627 年）。该塔为方形楼阁式空心砖塔，通高 36 米，保存完好。

Dagoba in Huiche Temple, Pucheng County

Built in the 1st year of Tang Emperor Zhenguan's reign (627 A. D.), it is in Pucheng Middle School, Pucheng County, Weinan City. The pagoda is a square pavilion-style hollow brick one with a height of 36 meters.

蒲城县敬母寺塔

位于渭南市蒲城县翔村镇敬母寺村。塔为三层楼阁式砖塔，高 10 米；一层为方形，底边长 4.5 米；二、三层为六边形。塔身刻有“文昌阁”“魁心楼”。

Pagoda in Jingmu Temple, Pucheng County

It is in Jingmusi Village, Xiangcun Town, Pucheng County, Weinan City. The pagoda is a three-storey pavilion-style brick one with a height of 10 meters. It is engraved with “Wen Chang Ge” and “Kui Xin Lou”.

蒲城县海源寺塔

位于渭南市蒲城县水丰镇温汤村。建于金代。塔为六边九层密檐式楼阁空心砖塔，现残存八层，残高 30 余米。

Pagoda in Haiyuan Temple, Pucheng County

Built in the Jin Dynasty (1115–1234 A. D.), it is in Wentang Village, Shuifeng Town, Pucheng County, Weinan City. The pagoda is a hollow brick tower with six-sided and nine-storey, and it has only eight-storey left with a residual height of about 30 meters currently.

富平县法源寺塔

位于渭南市富平县美原镇中心小学内。建于唐咸亨二年（671 年），历代均有修葺。塔为八边九层楼阁式空心砖塔，通高 27 米。每层仿木斗拱繁杂檐角向上翘，顶上置铁质瓶塔刹。

Pagoda in Fayuan Temple, Fuping County

Built in the 2rd year of Tang Emperor Xianheng's reign (671 A. D.) and repaired in successive dynasties, it is in the central primary school, Meiyuan Town, Fuping County, Weinan City. The pagoda is a hollow brick one with eight-sided and nine-storey, which is 27 meters high.

富平县万斛寺塔

位于渭南市富平县裕岭乡漫町村，建于唐。塔为方形七层楼阁式实心砖塔，通高 26.7 米，底边长 4 米。仿木结构施檐斗拱，造型庄重，工艺精巧。

Pagoda in Wanhu Temple, Fuping County

Built in the Tang Dynasty (618–907 A. D.), it is in Manding Village, Yuling Township, Fuping County, Weinan City. The pagoda is a square solid brick one with seven-storey, which is 26.7 meters high.

富平县圣佛寺塔

位于渭南市富平县城关镇尖角村。建于唐元和年间（806 年 ~ 820 年），明代重修。该寺已废，存塔为纪念碑性质。塔为八层楼阁式空心砖塔，通高 21 米。

Pagoda in Shengfo Temple, Fuping County

Built during Tang Emperor Yuanhe's reign (806–820 A. D.) and rebuilt in the Ming Dynasty (1368–1644A.D.), it is in Jianjiao Village, Chengguan Town, Fuping County, Weinan City. The pagoda is an eight-storey hollow brick one with a height of 21 meters.

延安市

Yan' an City

宝塔区岭山寺塔

位于延安市宝塔区宝塔山。俗称延安宝塔，建于明代。塔为八边九层楼阁式空心砖塔，每层叠涩出檐，高 44 米。底层南门额题“高潮碧落”四个字，北门额题“仰视红尘”四字。塔内有楼梯可攀登至顶。

Pagoda in Lingshan Temple, Baota District

Built in the Ming Dynasty (1368–1644 A. D.), it, also called Yan'an Pagoda, is in Baota Mountain, Baota District, Yan'an City. The pagoda is a hollow brick one with eight-sided and nine-storey, which is 44 meters high. It can be gone up to the top from the inside through stairs.

宝塔区清凉山琉璃塔

原位于延安市甘谷驿镇唐家坪村半山坡，1985年迁至延安市宝塔区清凉山上。建于明崇祯二年（1629年）。八边七层楼阁式实心琉璃塔，高6.25米，底层直径1.15米。塔身以蓝、绿、黄等色琉璃砖砌筑，上有各种小浮雕琉璃，如飞天、菩萨、佛、凤凰、朱雀、麒麟、鹿、马等。该塔系陕西省仅存的一座琉璃塔。

Glazed Pagoda in Qingliang Mountain, Baota District

Built in the 2rd year of Ming Emperor Chongzhen's reign (1629 A. D.), it is in Qingliang Mountain, Baota District, Yan'an City. The pagoda is a pavilion-style solid one with eight-sided and seven-storey, which is 6.25 meters high. It is built of colored glaze bricks, such as blue, green, yellow and so on, which is the only glazed pagoda remained in Shaanxi Province.

宝塔区清净正法明王如来佛塔

位于延安市宝塔区甘谷驿镇薛家沟村。又名薛家沟石塔，建于明万历三十五年（1607 年）。据塔铭知，该塔为僧德舟（1559 年 ~ 1607 年）的舍利塔。塔为六边十层实心石塔，现残存八层，高 4.82 米。塔基座为仰覆莲束腰须弥座，塔身各层均有塔铭并雕刻有龙、虎、宝相花、莲花等图案。

Buddha Stupa in Baota District

Built in the 35th year of Ming Emperor Wanli's reign (1607 A. D.), it is in Xuejiagou Village, Ganguyi Town, Baota District, Yan'an City. According to the inscription, the pagoda is the dagoba of monk Dezhou (1559–1607 A. D.). It is a solid stone pagoda with six-sided and ten-storey, which has eight-storey and is 4.82 meters high currently.

子长市普通塔

位于子长市安定镇姬家庄村西。又名惠善浮屠塔，具体修建年代不详，明洪武二十五年（1392 年）重修。塔为六边七层楼阁式实心石塔，高 9.17 米。塔第一层正面上方开龛，雕布袋和尚像；其他各层也有佛教造像。该塔身的石雕造像神态生动、古朴自然，在陕西本土塔中不多见，弥足珍贵。

Basic Tower in Zichang City

Located in the west of Jijiazhuang Village, Anding Town, Zichang City, it has unknown date of construction and it was rebuilt in the 25th year of Ming Emperor Hongwu's reign (1392 A. D.). The pagoda is a solid stone one with six-sided and seven-storey, which is 9.17 meters high. The stone statues on the tower body are vivid and plain, which are rare and precious among Shaanxi's pagodas.

子长市石宫寺塔

位于子长市安定镇钟山石窟山上。石窟山古塔林立、寺院延绵，是西北佛教传播重要发祥地之一。该塔建于明嘉靖二年（1523 年），清康熙年间（1662 年～1722 年）重修。六边五层楼阁式空心砖塔，通高 14.3 米，为清代风格。

Pagoda in Shigong Temple, Zichang City

Built in the 2rd year of Ming Emperor Jiajing's reign (1523 A. D.) and rebuilt during Qing Emperor Kangxi's reign (1662–1722 A. D.), it is in Zhongshan Grotto, Anding Town, Zichang City. Zhongshan Grotto is one of the important birthplaces for the spread of Buddhism in Northwest China. The Pagoda is a hollow brick one with six-sided and five-storey, which is 14.3 meters high.

延长县狗头山石塔

位于延安市延长县南河沟乡呼家村，建于清代。圆锥形三层石塔，高6.05米，塔身以块石砌筑，层间以层石出短檐，塔刹已毁。该塔为风水塔，风水塔在明清的陕北陕南地区较为常见。

Stone Pagoda in Goutou Mountain, Yanchang County

Built in the Qing Dynasty (1644–1911 A. D.), it is in Hujia Village, Nanhegou Township, Yanchang County, Yan'an City. The pagoda is a conical three-storey stone one with a height of 6 meters. It is Fengshui Pagoda, which is quite common in the Northern Shaanxi and Southern Shaanxi in the Ming (1368–1644 A. D.) and Qing (1644–1911 A. D.) Dynasties.

志丹县马家河塔

位于延安市志丹县永宁镇马家河村，又名白沙川塔。塔为千佛舍利塔，八边楼阁式空心砖塔，残存五层，高 5.6 米，每边长 1.2 米。塔上有砖雕马、花卉等图案。

Majiahe Pagoda in Zhidan County

It, also called Baishachuan Pagoda, is in Majiahe Village, Yongning Town, Zhidan County, Yan'an City. The pagoda is an eight-sided hollow brick one with a height of 5.6 meters, which has only five-storey left.

志丹县九塔湾明代塔群

位于延安市志丹县义正乡花石庵村。因此处原有九塔，故名九塔湾。现存 8 座塔，均为空心砖塔，其中方塔 2 座，八角塔 6 座，为宋代建筑。八角塔均为五层，高约 5.5 米。方塔一座为九层，高约 15 米；一座为五层，高约 9 米。

Pagodas in Jiuta Bay, Zhidan County

It is in Huashian Village, Yizheng Township, Zhidan County, Yan'an City. It is said that the place originally has nine pagodas, so it called Jiuta Bay. There are eight hollow brick pagodas left, including two square pagodas and six octagonal pagodas, which were all built in the Song Dynasty (960–1279 A. D.).

富县白骨塔

位于延安市富县张家湾镇油坊头村，建于清代。塔为方锥形实心砖石塔，“金”字塔形，通高 3.9 米，底边长 1.8 米，上题“白骨塔”三字。塔基为青石，条砖为塔身，通体呈灰白色。1844 年，清政府陕甘总督左宗棠镇压回民起义之后，差勇丁收捡骨骸，捡丢塔内，白骨塔由此得名。

Baigu Pagoda in Fu County

Built in the Qing Dynasty (1644–1911 A. D.), it is in Youfangtou Village, Zhangjiawan Town, Fu County, Yan'an City. The pagoda is a cone-shaped solid masonry one, shaped like a "pyramid", with a height of 3.9 meters. There are three characters on the pagoda "Bai Gu Ta". The tower footing is made of bluestone and its body, with off-white color, is made of strip bricks.

富县正昉公塔

位于延安市富县北道德乡梁子塬村西北，建于明代。八边四层楼阁式空心砖塔，残高 8 米，底边长 1.7 米。塔基为砖雕莲座，底层正南辟券门，二至四层正南辟券窗，其余各面均砖雕两层方龛，龛两侧饰砖雕莲花、牡丹、佛手等图案。平砖叠涩收顶，塔刹无存。

Zhengfanggong Pagoda in Fu County

Built in the Ming Dynasty (1368–1644 A. D.), it is in the northwest of Liangziyuan Village, Beidaode Township, Fu County, Yan'an City. The pagoda is a hollow brick one with eight-sided and four-storey, which has a residual height of 8 meters and its bottom side has 1.7 meters. The tower footing is made of tile carving with lotus-shape. There has arched door on the south of the ground floor and arched windows on the south of the second to fourth floors and other side are all made of tile carving with two layers of square niche.

富县福严院塔

位于延安市富县北道德乡东村，建于宋代。八边十三层密檐式空心砖塔，高 30.2 米。塔每层四面设券门，内辟方形小室。塔身用青砖磨沿对缝，以黄泥白灰加糯米汁砌筑而成，做工精细，为宋塔的巅峰之作。

Fuyanyuan Tower in Fu County

Built in the Song Dynasty (960–1279 A. D.), it is in Dong Village, Beidaode Township, Fu County, Yan'an City. The pagoda is a hollow brick one with eight-sided and thirteen-storey, which is 30.2 meters high. Its body, with fine workmanship, is paved with blue bricks, pasted by yellow mud, white ash with sticky rice juice, which is the peak of Song pagodas.

富县柏山寺塔

位于延安市富县直罗镇。又名直罗塔，具体建造年代不详。八边十一层密檐楼阁式实心砖塔，高 43.3 米，底周长 29.6 米，宋代建筑遗风。该塔收分柔和，秀丽端庄。

Pagoda in Baishan Temple, Fu County

Built in unknown date, it is in Zhiluo Town, Fu County, Yan'an City. The pagoda is a pavilion-style solid brick one with eight-sided and eleven-storey, which is 43.3 meters high with the architectural style of the Song Dynasty (960–1279 A. D.).

富县开元寺塔

位于延安市富县西北龟山半坡上，又名富县塔。开元寺建于唐开元年间（713年～741年），清代重修。塔为方形十一层楼阁式空心砖塔，高40米。平面呈四边四角形，面向正东，原建十三层，现残存十一层，顶层残缺。塔内有楼梯直通塔顶。

Pagoda in Kaiyuan Temple, Fu County

Built during Tang Emperor Kaiyuan's reign (713–741 A. D.), it, also called Fuxian Pagoda, is on the half slope of the Gui Mountain, northwest of Fu County, Yan'an City. Facing east, the pagoda was originally built on thirteen-storey, while now it has only eleven-storey left and the top floor is incomplete with a total height of 40 meters. It can be gone up to the top from the inside through stairs.

富县八卦寺明代塔群

位于延安市富县张家湾镇八卦寺村，建于明代。相传该处原有八塔，故称八卦寺。原寺院已毁，现存砖塔三座。左塔高 9.7 米，八边密檐楼阁式实心砖塔，残存八层；中塔高 9.5 米，方形八层檐实心砖塔；右塔高 10 米，八边楼阁实心砖塔，残存八层。整个塔群造型简洁美观、古朴庄严。

Pagodas in Bagua Temple, Fu County

Built in the Ming Dynasty (1368–1644 A. D.), it is in Baguasi Village, Zhangjiawan Town, Fu County, Yan'an City. It is said that the place originally has eight pagodas, so it called Bagua Temple. The original temple has been destroyed and there are only three brick towers left. The pagodas are simple and elegant in appearance with plain and solemn style.

洛川县万凤塔

位于延安市洛川县土基镇鄜城村。俗称兴国寺塔、鄜城古塔，始建于唐，宋、明均有多次修葺。八边十三层密檐楼阁式空心砖塔，通高 42 米，底边长 3.3 米，塔刹无存，内有木梯可通顶。

Wanfeng pagoda in Luochuan County

Built in the Tang Dynasty (618–907 A. D.) and repaired several times in both Song (960–1279 A. D.) and Ming (1368–1644 A. D.) dynasties, it is in Fucheng Village, Tuji Town, Luochuan County, Yan'an City. The pagoda is a hollow brick one with eight-sided and thirteen-storey, which is 42 meters high. A wooden ladder in it can be climbed to the top.

洛川县土塔

位于延安市洛川县槐北镇东头村，建于清代，为村里的风水塔。高 6 米，保存完好。土塔因地制宜、就地取材，在陕北地区盛行。

Earthen Tower in Luochuan County

Built in the Qing Dynasty (1644–1911 A. D.), it, the Fengshui Pagoda of the village, is in Dongtou Village, Huaibei Town, Luochuan County, Yan'an City. The pagoda, well preserved, is 6 meters high.

宜川县文昌阁塔

位于延安市宜川县阁楼镇柴村内。又名柴村塔，建于清代。方形锥形实心砖塔，通高6.35米。以碎石片砌筑成方形塔基，正南面开一方龛，方龛上题刻“文昌阁”三字。文昌塔是旧时为祝愿学子们中举而建，在陕北，几乎每个村落庙宇中都有“文昌君”的供奉。

Wenchangge Pagoda in Yichuan County

Built in the Qing Dynasty (1644–1911 A. D.), it is in Chai Village, Gelou Town, Yichuan County, Yan'an City. The pagoda is a square cone-shaped solid brick one with a height of 6.35 meters. Wenchang Pagoda was built in Northern Shaanxi for wishing students' success in the past. Therefore, almost every temple in villages has "Wenchang Jun" enshrined in it.

宜川县文峰塔

位于延安市宜川县新河镇下北赤村。据塔的建筑风格看为清代建筑。塔为六边五层楼阁式实心砖塔，高 9.6 米，底层边长 1.3 米，石块砌筑塔基。

Wenfeng Pagoda in Yichuan County

Located in Xiabeichi Village, Xinhe Town, Yichuan County, Yan'an City, it is Qing (1644–1911 A. D.) architectural style. The pagoda is a solid brick one with six-sided and five-storey, which is 9.6 meters high.

宜川县风水塔

位于延安市宜川县楼阁镇下汾川村，为该村的风水塔。方锥形实心砖塔，通高10米，底边长2.3米，块石砌筑塔基。该塔与其他不同的是塔顶一层上出檐加菱角作装饰，平砖攒尖收顶，塔刹无存。

Fengshui Pagoda in Yichuan County

It, the Fengshui Pagoda of the village, is in Fenchuan Village, Louge Town, Yichuan County, Yan'an City. The pagoda is a cone-shaped solid brick one with a height of 10 meters, which has 2.3 meters of bottom side. The tower footing is made of a whole piece of stone.

黄龙县文峰塔

位于延安市黄龙县柏峪镇王庄村西，为该村的风水塔。圆锥形石塔，残高6米，底层周长11.3米。塔身有券龛，塔顶已残。

Wenfeng Pagoda in Huanglong County

It, the Fengshui Pagoda of the village, is in the west of Wangzhuang Village, Baiyu Town, Huanglong County, Yan'an City. The pagoda is a conical stone one with a residual height of 6 meters. Its body has arched niche and the top of the pagoda has been damaged.

汉中市
Hanzhong City

汉台区净明寺塔

位于汉中市汉台区、东关净明寺（原东塔小学校舍）。塔为方形密檐式实心砖塔，原为十三层，现存十一层，高16.5米，从艺术风格看应为宋塔。

Pagoda in Jingming Temple, Hantai District

It is in Hantai District, Hanzhong City. The pagoda, with Song (960–1279 A. D.) architectural style, is a square solid brick one with a height of 16.5 meter, which has eleven-storey left.

南郑区柳树沟舍利墓塔

位于汉中市南郑区青柳村。塔为六边三层多宝塔式舍利塔，已残，高3.93米，刻有花卉，塔刹已无。

Sarira Tomb Pagodas in Willow Ditch, Nanzheng District

It is in Qingliu Village, Nanzheng District, Hanzhong City. The pagoda, damaged now, is a dagoba with six-sided and three-storey, which is 3.93 meters high.

南郑区康家坝舍利塔

位于汉中市南郑区小海南乡康家坝村，建于清道光十六年（1836 年）。塔为六边五层楼阁式舍利石塔，高 3.73 米。塔身刻有浅浮雕仙鹤、渔、鼓、花草等图案，塔刹无存。

Dagoba in Kangjia Dam, Nanzheng District

Built in the 16th year of Qing Emperor Daoguang's reign (1836 A. D.), it is in Tangjiabei Village, Xiaohainan Township, Nanzheng District, Hanzhong City. The pagoda is a sarira stone one with a height of 3.73 meters. Its body is engraved with various patterns in bas-relief, such as cranes, fish, drums, flowers and plants and so on.

洋县开明寺塔

位于汉中市洋县开明寺内，又名关寺塔，始建于唐开元十五年（727 年），宋庆元元年（1195 年）重修。塔为方形十三层密檐式实心砖塔，高 31.2 米。塔身各层具有券门，佛龛内有石雕佛像，各层塔檐角上均有风铃。

Pagoda in Kaiming Temple, Yang County

Built in the 15th year of Tang Emperor Kaiyuan's reign (727 A. D.) and rebuilt in the 1st year of Song Emperor Qingyuan's reign (1195 A. D.), it, also called Pagoda in Guan Temple, is in Kaiming Temple, Yang County, Hanzhong City. The pagoda is a square solid brick one with thirteen-storey, which is 31.2 meters.

洋县华阳古塔

位于汉中市洋县华阳河西岸台上，建于清乾隆三十年（1765年）。塔为方形五层楼阁式实心砖塔，高16米。塔身无装饰，每层都有券门。由下而上逐层收缩，至顶呈尖坡形。该塔主要用来震慑洪水，安民保业。

Ancient pagoda in Huayang Town, Yang County

Built in the 30th year of Qing Emperor Qianlong's reign (1765 A. D.), it is in the west bank of Huayang River, Yang County, Hanzhong City. The pagoda is a square five-storey solid brick one with a height of 16 meters. It is mainly used to owe floods and guarantee people's daily work and life.

西乡县圆通寺舍利塔

位于汉中市西乡县西河口镇和平村。建筑年代不详。塔为八边三层石塔，高 8 米。

Dagoba in Yuantong Temple, Xixiang County

Built in unknown date, it is in Heping Village, Xihekou Town, Xixiang County, Hanzhong City. The pagoda is an eight-sided three-storey stone one with a height of 8 meters.

勉县万寿寺塔

位于汉中市勉县，始建于明万历年间（1573 年～ 1620 年）。塔为六边十一层空心砖塔，高 24.85 米，塔基周长 17.4 米，直径 6 米。塔身自下而上逐层递减，结构严谨、造型美观。

Pagoda in Temple of Longevity, Mian County

Built during Ming Emperor Wanli's reign (1573–1620 A. D.), it is in Mian County, Hanzhong City. The pagoda is a hollow brick one with six-sided and eleven-storey, which is 24.85 meters high.

略阳县福地祥云塔

位于汉中市略阳县城南山上。又名略阳南山塔，建于清道光三十年（1850 年）。塔为六边七层楼阁式空心砖塔，通高 24 米，底层边长 2.35 米。

Fudixiangyun Pagoda in Lueyang County

Built in the 30th year of Qing Emperor Daoguang's reign (1850 A. D.), it is in Chengnan Mountain, Lueyang County, Hanzhong City. The pagoda is a hollow brick one with six-sided and seven-storey, which is 24 meters.

略阳县铁佛寺塔

位于汉中市略阳县青泥河乡铁佛寺村。该塔深藏山野之中，原寺无存，塔建于明正德十三年（1518 年）。塔为方形三层楼阁式实心砖塔，通高 8 米，底边长 2.42 米。塔基分明，顶层为石板凿成，平砖出檐短薄，歇山式顶塔，属于风水塔。

Pagoda in Tiefo Temple, Lueyang County

Built in the 13th year of Ming Emperor Zhengde's reign (1518 A. D.), it is in Tiefosi Village, Qingnihe Township, Lueyang County, Hanzhong City. The pagoda, belonged to Fengshui Pagoda, is a square three-storey solid brick one with a height of 8 meters.

镇巴县至宝塔

位于汉中市镇巴县，建于清光绪五年（1879 年）。该塔为清净寺觉灵大师之墓塔，共七层，由大块石头修筑而成。

Zhibao Pagoda in Zhenba County

Built in the 5th year of Qing Emperor Guangxu's reign (1879 A. D.), it is in Zhenba County, Hanzhong City. The pagoda, made of large stone, is Tomb Pagoda of Master Jueling in Qingjing Temple.

佛坪县了贤和尚墓塔

位于汉中市佛坪县东岳殿镇石印沟村，建于清咸丰年间（1851 年～ 1861 年）。塔为方形舍利石塔，通高 2.7 米，底边宽 1.45 米。

Liaoxian Monk Tomb Pagoda in Foping County

Built during Qing Emperor Xianfeng's reign (1851–1861 A. D.), it is in Shiyingou Village, Dongyuedian Town, Foping County, Hanzhong City. The pagoda is a square sarira stone one with a height of 2.7 meters.

榆林市
Yulin City

榆阳区凌霄塔

位于榆林市榆阳区镇远门南。又名榆阳寺塔，建于明万历年间（1573 年 ~ 1620 年）。八边十三层密檐楼阁式空心砖塔，高 43 米，石砌塔基。塔每层均悬挂风铃，出檐较短具明代砖塔特征。该塔为榆林市地标性建筑之一，为“榆林八景”之一。

Lingxiao Pagoda in Yuyang District

Built during Ming Emperor Shenzong's reign(1573-1620A.D.), it, which also called Yuyang Temple, is in the south of Zhenyuan gate, Yuyang District, Yulin City. Its footing was built of stones. The pagoda, 43meters high, is one of the landmark buildings in Yulin city, listed as one of "the Eight Attractions of Yulin City".

榆阳区古塔寺塔

位于榆林市榆阳区古塔镇古塔村。建于明成化年间（1465年～1487年），清光绪二十一年（1895年）补修。八边七层实心砖塔，通高10.7米。塔基以石片砌成，第二、七层各有券龛，檐角微翘，檐下有砖仿木斗拱，塔上有砖雕花卉、葵花等装饰。

Pagoda in Guta Temple, Yuyang District

Built during Ming Emperor Chenghua's reign (1465–1487 A. D.) and repaired in the 21th of Qing Emperor Guangxu's reign (1895 A. D.), it is in Guta Village, Guta Town, Yuyang District, Yulin City. The pagoda is a solid brick one with eight-sided and seven-storey, which is 10.7 meters high. The tower footing is made of flags and the pagoda is decorated by bricks with flower-shape, such as sunflowers and so on.

横山区鸿门寺响铃塔

位于榆林市横山区塔湾镇西南 1 千米处。据历代县志记载，该塔建于元泰定年间（1324 年～1328 年）。密檐式砖塔，空心，平面呈八角形，第一层为石片砌筑，以上为砖构成，共十一层，高 27 米。塔檐每角原悬有风铃，故名响铃塔。

Xiangling Pagoda in Hongmen Temple, Hengshan District

According to the records of county annals in past dynasties, it, built during Yuan Emperor Taiding's reign (1324–1328 A. D.), is on the 1 kilometer southeast of Tawan Town, Hengshan District, Yulin City. The pagoda is a dense-eaves brick one with eleven-storey and 27 meters high. Every corner of the eaves was originally hung with wind bells, so, It was formerly called Xiangling Pagoda.

横山区王皮庄响铃塔

位于榆林市横山区赵石畔镇王皮庄村，又名王皮庄佛塔，建于清代。现存三层多宝塔式石塔，通高 5.2 米，基石八边形，塔基上刻有莲、须弥座。三层塔身均为整块石料雕琢而成，八棱石雕加仿木建结构四流水塔檐。有莲花、牡丹、凤鸟等图案作修饰，造型别致。

Xiangling Pagoda in Wangpizhuang Village, Hengshan District

Built in the Qing Dynasty (1644–1911 A. D.), it is in Wangpizhuang Village, Zhaoshipan Town, Hengshan District, Yulin City. The pagoda is a three-storey stone one with the shape of Duobao Pagoda, which is 5.2 meters high now. Its body is carved from a single block of stone with unique shapes, such as lotus, peonies, phoenixes and so on.

横山区接引寺塔

位于榆林市横山区波罗镇的古堡山上。山上有接引寺，始建于唐贞观二十二年（648 年）。该塔建于明成化年间（1465 年～1487 年），高 12 米，为八边九层密檐式砖塔，有仿木斗拱，呈现出清秀俊美的艺术特征。

Pagoda in Jieyin Temple, Hengshan District

Built during Ming Emperor Chenghua's reign (1465–1487 A. D.), it is in Gubao Mountain, Boluo Town, Hengshan District, Yulin City. The pagoda is an eight-sided and nine-storey brick one with a height of 12 meters, which is quite delicate and pretty.

横山区法云寺塔群

位于榆林市横山区殿市镇五龙山村。五龙山村历史悠久，塔群位于山上的古庙中，建或重修均有。其中一塔高 2.07 米，边长 1.14 米。另一舍利塔位于古庙北侧同为六边形弥座，塔高约 6 米。

Pagodas in Fayun Temple, Hengshan District

It is in Wulongshan Village, Dianshi Town, Hengshan District, Yulin City. Wulongshan Village has a long history. The pagodas are in the ancient temple on the mountain, some of which are under construction or rebuilt.

横山区清凉寺喇嘛塔

位于榆林市横山区党岔镇胡新窑村清凉寺后的黄土坡上，又名林孝塔。该塔为砖塔，高11米。从外形看，属典型的喇嘛式砖塔，塔基有片石砌筑而成，塔身以砖砌成，八边形须弥座，每边长1.4米，雕饰有莲花、凤鸟、云纹、麒麟等图案。

Stupa in Qingliang Temple, Hengshan District

It, also called Linxiao Pagoda, is in Huxinyao Village, Dangcha Town, Hengshan District, Yulin City. The pagoda is a brick one with a height of 11 meters. From its appearance, it is a typical lama-style brick pagoda. The tower footing is built of slab stones, while its body is built of bricks.

府谷县黄甫石塔

位于榆林市府谷县黄甫镇，建于明代。六边五层楼阁式石造像塔，以当地砂岩雕凿而成，残高 5 米，每边长 1.25 米。该塔由各种花卉浮雕、文字等修饰，塔内有坐佛一尊，风化严重。

Stone Pagoda in Huangpu Town, Fugu County

Built in the Ming Dynasty (1368–1644 A. D.), it is in Huangpu Town, Fugu County, Yulin City. The six-sided and five-storey stone pagoda is carved from local sandstones, with a residual height of 5 meters and 1.25 meters high of each side.

绥德县合龙山塔

位于榆林市绥德县张家砭镇五里湾村，建于明万历十八年（1590年）。塔为八边九层密檐楼阁式空心砖塔，高17米，底边宽2.4米。塔基石砌，塔各层均有券门龛，各层檐角仿木斗拱飞檐上翘，具有很强的装饰性，极具特色。塔内木梯已毁。

Pagoda in Helong Mountain, Suide County

Built in the 18th year of Ming Emperor Wanli's reign (1590 A. D.), it is in Wuliwan Village, Zhangjiabian Town, Suide County, Yulin City. The pagoda is a hollow brick one with eight-sided and nine-storey, which is 17 meters high. The tower footing is built of barnacles, and it has arched niche in each floor.

绥德县兴善寺普通塔

位于榆林市绥德县满堂川镇赵家铺村义水河北岸。该塔位于兴善寺中，塔身有铭文“旨大明景泰二年（1451 年）岁在辛未孟夏己巳朔十一日己卯吉时立”。六层经幢式石塔，高 10 米，塔身每层由整块石料雕琢，依次套接而成，中间有龙的雕琢图案。

Basic Tower in Xingshan Temple, Suide County

Built in the 2rd year of Ming Emperor Jingtai's reign (1451 A. D.), it is in Xingshan Temple, the northern bank of the Yishui River, Zhaojiapu Village, Mantangchuan Town, Suide County, Yulin City. The pagoda is a six-storey stone one with a height of 10 meters.

米脂县天王塔

位于榆林市米脂县郭兴庄乡天王塔村。又名祖师庙塔，从风格看为明代建筑。原为六边七层楼阁式实心砖塔，高 12 米，现存四层多，残高约 9 米。塔基一层宽大，以上逐渐锐减，塔面无装饰，最上面一层有券龛。

Tianwang Pagoda in Mizhi County

It, also called Zushi Temple pagoda, is in Tianwangta Village, Guoxingzhuang Township, Mizhi County, Yulin City, which is a typical Ming (1368–1644 A. D.) architectural style. The pagoda was originally a solid brick one with six-sided and seven-storey, which is 12 meters high. It is four-storey with a residual height of about 9 meters currently.

佳县凌云塔

位于榆林市佳县城东县体育场内。当地亦称雁塔，建于明万历三十九年（1611 年）。塔为八边七层楼阁式空心砖塔，通高 26.4 米。石砌塔基，内设木梯可攀登。塔身塔檐平砖砌筑，无雕刻装饰，保存完好。

LinYun Pagoda in Jia County

Built in the 39th year of Ming Emperor Wanli's reign (1611 A. D.), it, called Yan Pagoda locally, is in Jia County, Yulin City. The pagoda is a hollow brick one with eight-sided and seven-storey, which is 26.4 meters high. The tower footing is built of barnacles and a wooden ladder in it can be climbed.

安康市

Ankang City

汉滨区牛蹄岭兴贤塔

位于安康市汉滨区牛蹄岭上，建于清道光年间（1821年～1850年）。塔共七层，高约23米，底层宽约4米，塔顶宽约1.5米。该塔是国内保存最完整、高度最高的纯石塔。

Xingxian Pagoda in Niuti Ridge, Hanbin District

Built during Qing Emperor Daoguang's reign (1821–1850 A. D.), it is in Niuti Ridge, Hanbin District, Ankang City. The pagoda has seven-storey with a height of about 23 meters, which is the most complete and highest stone one in China.

汉滨区奠安塔

位于安康市汉滨区张滩镇奠安村，建于民国。塔为方形七层楼阁式砖塔，通高28米，底边长5米。塔身各层有券门或券窗，一层题刻“奠安塔”三字。各层檐角上翘，为卷云装饰，四角攒顶，上置宝瓶式塔刹。

Dian'an Pagoda in Hanbin District

Built in the Repubilc of China (1912–1949 A. D.), it is in Dian'an Village, Zhangtan Town, Hanbin District, Ankang City. The pagoda is a square seven-storey brick one with a height of 28 meters. There are arched doors or arched windows on each floor of the pagoda, and the first floor of it engraved with three words "Dian An Ta".

汉阴县文峰塔

位于安康市汉阴县城关镇，建于清同治十二年（1873 年）。塔筑于明城墙东南角隅垣上，是当时县令及地方绅士为“文出卧龙”而捐资修建的。塔为六边五层楼阁式空心砖塔，高 23.6 米，底边长 3.8 米。

Wenfeng Pagoda in Hanyin County

Built in the 12th year of Qing Emperor Tongzhi's reign (1873 A. D.), it is in Chengguan Town, Hanyin County, Ankang City. The pagoda is a pavilion-style hollow brick one with six-sided and five-storey, which is 23.6 meters high and bottom side is 3.8 meters.

石泉县吴家寨墓塔

位于安康市石泉县绕镇红莲村。俗称将军塔墓，为南宋抗金名将吴玠（1093年～1139年）之衣冠冢。塔为八边三层楼阁式空心塔，高5米，方形，片石垒砌。

Tomb Pagoda in Wujiazhai, Shiquan County

It, also called the Tomb Pagoda of General, is in Honglian Village, Rao Town, Shiquan County, Ankang City, which is the cenotaph of Wu Jie (1093–1139 A. D.), a famous general fighting with the Jin Dynasty (1115–1234A.D.) for the Southern Song Dynasty (1127–1279A.D.). The pagoda is a hollow one with eight-sided and three-storey, which is 5 meters high.

宁陕县观音山舍利塔

位于安康市宁陕县新矿镇，又名多宝塔舍利塔。三层塔，通高5米。塔身通体浮雕花卉，套石连接。顶为莲花宝座，做工精细。

Dagoba in Guanyin Mountain, Ningshan County

It is in Xinkuang Town, Ningshan County, Ankang City, with three-storey and a height of 5 meters. The body is engraved with relief flowers, which has fine workmanship.

紫阳县报恩寺塔

位于安康市紫阳县房镇贾家坪村，建于清咸丰年间（1851年~1861年）。塔为六边七层楼阁式砖塔，高19.5米，底边长2.3米。

Pagoda in Baoen Temple, Ziyang County

Built during Qing Emperor Xianfeng's reign (1851–1861 A. D.), it is in Jiajiaping Village, Fang Town, Ziyang County, Ankang City. The pagoda is a brick one with six-sided and seven-storey, which is 19.5 meters high.

平利县莲花台僧人墓塔

位于安康市平利县洛河镇狮子坝莲花台村。塔为清代建筑样式，四层砖石舍利塔，高 3.8 米。底层为圆形，一至三层为块石砌筑，最上层为青砖砌筑。

Monk Tomb Pagoda in Lianhuatai, Pingli County

With Qing (1644–1911 A. D.) architectural style, it is in Lianhuatai Village and Shiziba Village, Luohe Town, Pingli County, Ankang City. The pagoda is a four-storey dagoba, which is made of bricks with a height of 3.8 meters.

平利县观音堂僧人墓塔

位于安康市平利县大贵乡张家湾村。塔为六边三层楼阁式空心石舍利塔，高5.2米，底层长1.5米。

Monk Tomb Pagoda in Guanyintang, Pingli County

It is in Zhangjiawan Village, Dagui Township, Pingli County, Ankang City. The pagoda is a hollow stone-made dagoba with six-sided and three-storey, which is 5.2 meters high.

平利县三佛洞舍利塔

位于安康市平利县中坪乡龙儿沟村，建于清道光七年（1827年）。塔为六边五层楼阁式实心舍利塔，高 9 米，底径 2.6 米。

Dagoba in Sanfodong, Pingli County

Built in the Qing Emperor Daoguang's reign (1827 A. D.), it is in Longergou Village, Zhongping Township, Pingli County, Ankang City. The pagoda is a dagoba with six-sided and five-storey, which is 9 meters high.

旬阳县灵岩寺文星塔

位于安康市旬阳县城关镇王家山村，建于清光绪元年（1875年）。塔为六边五层砖石塔，高7.5米，底层直径2.1米。一至四层为石砌实心，面涂白灰、墨勾砖缝；第五层为砖砌空心，内有魁星点斗木雕一尊。

Wenxing Pagoda in Lingyan Temple, Lingyan Temple, Xunyang County

Built in the 1st year of Qing Emperor Guangxu's reign (1875 A. D.), it is in Wangjiashan Village, Chengguan Town, Xunyang County, Ankang City. The pagoda is a masonry one with six-sided and five-storey, which is 7.5 meters high.

旬阳县旗杆山文星塔

位于安康市旬阳县城关镇烂滩沟村，建于清光绪二十九年（1903年）。塔为六边五层砖塔，通高9.5米，底层边长3.4米，顶层有佛龛。

Wenxing Pagoda in Qigan Mountain, Xunyang County

Built in the 29th year of Qing Emperor Guangxu's reign (1903 A. D.), it is in Lantangou Village, Chengguan Town, Xunyang County, Ankang City. The pagoda is a six-sided five-storey brick one, with a height of 9.5 meters and a niche on the top.

旬阳县东宝塔

位于安康市旬阳县羊山乡东庵村。俗称东庵红安寺塔，建于明正德年间（1506 年 ~ 1521 年），为古红安寺遗迹之一。塔为六边五层实心砖塔，通高 11.02 米。塔通体为仿木结构，每级各面均有檐头、角脊、斗拱和门窗装饰，构造精巧、大方。

Dongbao Pagoda in Xunyang County

Built during Ming Emperor Zhengde's reign (1506–1521 A. D.), it is in Dong'an Village, Yangshan Township, Xunyang County, Ankang City. The pagoda is a solid brick one with six-sided and five-storey, which is 11.02 meters high.

白河县蜡烛山石塔

位于安康市白河县卡子镇下湾界岭村。塔为明代建筑样式，六边五层楼阁式空心石塔，高 8 米，上有浮雕花卉于石条上。

Stone Pagoda in Lazhu Mountain, Baihe County

With Ming (1368–1644 A. D.) architectural style, it is in Jieling Village, Kazi Town, Baihe County, Ankang City. The pagoda is a hollow stone one with six-sided and five-storey, which is 8 meters high.

白河县双塔寺塔

位于安康市白河县双河镇双塔寺村。双塔寺塔现只存一塔，塔为明代建筑样式，六边四层楼阁式实心砖塔，高 9.5 米。塔檐、塔角有仿木砖雕斗拱、龙头，塔体二层以上均有券门。

Pagoda in Shuangta Temple, Baihe County

With Ming (1368–1644 A. D.) architectural style, it is in Shuangtasi Village, Shuanghe Town, Baihe County, Ankang City. The Pagoda has only one left, which is a six-sided and four-storey solid brick one with a height of 9.5 meters.

商洛市
Shangluo City

商州区东龙山大塔

位于商洛市商州区城关镇东龙山村。又名南塔，建于明万历十九年（1591 年）。塔为八边九层密檐楼阁式空心砖塔，高 31.5 米，底边长 4.2 米，塔身有券门。

Big Pagoda in Donglong Mountain, Shangzhou District

Built in the 19th year of Ming Emperor Wanli's reign (1591 A.D.), it, also called Nan Pagoda, is in Donglongshan Village, Chengguan Town, Shangzhou District, Shangluo City. The pagoda is a hollow brick one with eight-sided and nine-storey, which is 31.5 meters high.

商州区东龙山小塔

位于商洛市商州区城关镇东龙山村。又名北塔，该塔与东龙山大塔几乎为同一时期建设。八边七层密檐楼阁式空心砖塔，高19.6米，底层边长2.66米。塔上雕有八卦、莲花灯、花卉的浮雕图案。

Small Pagoda in Donglong Mountain, Shangzhou District

Built in the same time of the Big Pagoda in Donglong Mountain, it, also called Bei Pagoda, is in Donglongshan Village, Chengguan Town, Shangzhou District, Shangluo City. The pagoda is a hollow brick one with eight-sided and seven-storey, which is 19.6 meters high.

丹凤县冠山石塔

位于商洛市丹凤县鸡冠山。建筑年代不详。塔为六边七级实心石塔，高7米，表面饰有莲纹、乳钉等图案。

Stone Pagoda in Guan Mountain, Danfeng County

Built in unknown date, it is in Jiguan Mountain, Danfeng County, Shangluo City. The pagoda is a solid stone one with six-sided and seven-storey, which is 7 meters high.

丹凤县八龙庙舍利塔

位于商洛市丹凤县土门镇八龙庙村。建筑年代不详。塔为典型的喇嘛式石塔，高 4.2 米。

Dagoba in Balong Temple, Danfeng County

Built in unknown date, it is in Balongmiao Village, Tumen Town, Danfeng County, Shangluo City. The pagoda is a typical lama-style stone one with a height of 4.2 meters.

山阳县丰阳塔

位于商洛市山阳县城的苍龙山。始建于唐永徽三年（652年），宋、清及民国有修复。塔为六边九层密檐式砖塔，高21米，底层边长2.54米。全塔以红砖垒成，工艺独特，下层最高，上层最短，各层有不同的砖砌图饰。

Fengyang Pagoda in Shanyang County

Built in the 3rd year of Tang Emperor Yonghui's reign (652 A. D.) and repaired in the Song (960–1279 A. D.) and Qing (1644–1911 A. D.) Dynasties and the Republic of China (1912–1949 A. D.), it is in Canglong Mountain, Shanyang County, Shangluo City. The pagoda is a brick one with six-sided and nine-storey, which is 21 meters high. It is built of red bricks with unique style.

山阳县庙沟石塔

位于商洛市山阳县色河铺镇庙沟村。该塔从艺术风格看具明代建筑特征，由整石套雕而成。三层多宝塔式舍利塔，高 4.5 米。

Stone Dagoba in Miaogou Village, Shanyang County

With Ming (1368–1644 A. D.) architectural style, it is in Miaogou Village, Sehepu Town, Shanyang County, Shangluo City. The pagoda is an over three-storey dagoba with a height of 4.5 meters.

镇安县塔云山念功塔

位于商洛市镇安县柴坪镇塔云山，建于清。塔为六边三层道士塔，通高 6.5 米，底层边长 1.5 米，由页岩质石材砌成。

Niangong Pagoda in Tayun Mountain, Zhen'an County

Built in the Qing Dynasty (1644–1911 A. D.), it is in Tayun Mountain, Chaiping Town, Zhen'an County, Shangluo City. The pagoda is a Pagoda of Taoist Priest with six-sided and three-storey, which is 6.5 meters high.